# ALIVE

by Mahima Gupta and Isha Shingari

*Dedicated to those who unwaveringly maintain their spirit and perseverance, regardless of the circumstances.*

# Contents

# Acknowledgement

We extend our deepest gratitude to all who have supported us on this poetic journey. First and foremost, we thank the almighty for countless blessings and for being the anchor that helped us steady in every storm of our lives.

We would also like to thank **Mr. Bismay Mohanty** and **Mr. Satya Ranjan Swain** for their contribution behind the scenes. This book was not possible without their efforts.

<u>*Mahima Gupta*</u>

With profound gratitude I extend my heart-felt Thanks to everyone who kept me 'Alive' when everything seemed to be falling apart.

This was not possible without the unconditional love and support of my parents **Manju Gupta** and **Malchand Gupta**. Thank You for believing in me and providing me strength to keep going even in the darkest of time.

Thanks to my younger brother **Arpit Khandelwal** for being a constant source of strength. You have brought me back to life with your boundless love and encouragement.

My heartfelt gratitude to my Mentor **Mr. Narendra Baidh** who has played a crucial role in steering me through the toughest times. Thank You for illuminating my path through your wisdom and insights.

My deepest gratitude to my school buddy and unpaid therapist **Rajani Jagarwal** who has always been a beacon of hope. The moment I felt lost in life you bought me back with your understanding and support. I am extremely grateful for your presence in my life.

My special thanks to my coach **Mr. Pujan Ghosh** for his patience and belief in my capabilities has always empowered me to face adversity. Sir, your lessons were always beyond training and have instilled me a sense of confidence and inner strength.

I would like to thank my colleague and mentor **Mr. Rakesh Yadav** who has always been a constant support and a source of inspiration. Thanks to my colleague **Mr. Abhishek Das** for his trust in my abilities and valuable insights which have been instrumental in my professional growth.

Thanks to my sister in law and friend **Saloni Gupta**, my unbiological parents **Nirmala Gupta** and **Satya Prakash Gupta**, my support systems **Kanika Gupta**, **Prateek Khandelwal** and **Aanchal Khandelwal**, my friends **Sonali Vyas**, **Priya Goyal**, **Garima Sharma** and **Khushboo Sharma** who were always a call away when I needed them. I would like to express my gratitude to my brother and friend **Bismay Mohanty** who has always been a pillar of my strength throughout the journey.

Each of you has played a pivotal role in my life. This book is a celebration of my experience and triumphs over the depth of depression.

## *Isha Shingari*

I extend my deepest gratitude to all who have supported me on this poetic journey. To my beloved family -   my parents, **Ramesh Shingari** and **Sangeeta Shingari**, whose wisdom and love inspired many of the verses in this collection.

Special thanks to my husband, **Sumit Sharma**, whose unwavering support fuels my creative spirit every day. And to our son, **Rayaan**, whose laughter and innocence fill our home with warmth and joy beyond measure.

To my co-author, **Mahima Gupta**, your creativity and collaboration have enriched this journey in ways I could never have imagined.

A heartfelt thanks to my family and friends, your steadfast love and encouragement have been the bedrock of my creativity. I owe a debt of gratitude to the enchanting city of Jaipur, my hometown, for painting my childhood with vivid hues that continue to inspire my writing today.

Additionally, the distance between Canada and India has inspired me to write even more fervently, turning separation into a source of creative energy.

Canada, with its serene landscapes and welcoming spirit, has been a nurturing ground for my creativity, allowing me to reflect and write with a heart full of gratitude.

Lastly, dear readers, I thank you for embracing my poetry with open hearts. May these words resonate with you, offering solace, introspection, and a glimpse into the mosaic of emotions that weave through our lives.

# Preface

In the whirlwind of life's adventures, amid the chaos of adulthood and the challenges of time zones, there exists a bond so strong it defies both distance and the inevitability of growing up.

Mahima and Isha, are friends since dinosaurs roamed the Earth  ( we've  lost count of the years because, let's face it, who wants to feel older?), found ourselves on opposite ends of the globe—Mahima in the colorful chaos of India and Isha navigating the maple syrup trails of Canada.

Our friendship, like fine wine (or maybe more like those questionable school lunches we survived together), has aged beautifully despite the miles that separate us. Imagine two friends, Mahima and Isha, separated by oceans and time zones for three long years. It was during one of those magical late-night talks, fueled by caffeine and nostalgia, that the idea for this collection was born. Isha, jet-lagged from her flight to India, and Mahima, wide awake on her end, found themselves transported back to the days of schoolyard secrets and shared dreams.

In the midst of laughter and tears, amidst the chaos of catching up and reminiscing, they realized how writing this book together could bridge the physical distance and reignite the spark of their friendship. A poetic journey back to the playgrounds of our youth, where we could swing high and dream higher.

Through "ALIVE," we embark on a hilarious and heartwarming expedition to rediscover the laughter, the secrets, and the sheer unadulterated mischief that defined our friendship. Each poem is a love letter to those moments we hold dear, an ode to the girlhood escapades that shaped us into the fierce, fabulous women we are today.

We would like to Thank You for choosing to read this book. 'Alive' is a celebration of friendship and expressing gratitude to all those who stood by us in difficult times. This book also serves as a triumphant celebration of overcoming depression and testament of indomitable human spirit. Through these pages we acknowledge the silent battle fought and resilience required to emerge victorious. It is also important to thank all those who lend their strength and compassion when we need it the most.

You are ALIVE because that bittersweet childhood memory brings a smile on your face. You are ALIVE by the intricate bond that ties us together. You are ALIVE because you have strength and determination to rise above the challenges and hope that ignites your soul.

Each poem is a glimpse into the human spirit, celebrating the beauty, resilience, and complexity of our journeys.

**Reminiscence** reflects on the formative years of a little girl growing up in a vibrant home, where memories and dreams interlace to inspire her as she matures. **Mothers and Daughters** is a timeless ode to the enduring bond between a mother and daughter, encapsulating the love, wisdom, and joy they share.

**Childhood Memories** paints a poetic journey through the joys of youth. A **Daughter's Love Across the Seas** expresses a daughter's deep longing for her distant father, highlighting the unbreakable bond they share.

**Silence** drawn from personal ordeal, portraying the haunting quietness and isolating experience of despair and arduous journey towards recovery. **Karma and Forgiveness** delves into divine justice and spiritual growth that emerges from embracing forgiveness.

**From Bump to Toddler Steps** is A Mother's Journey tenderly narrates the evolution of motherhood, from pregnancy to watching a child grow.

**Hope** critique upon people's superficial assessment rather than understanding. Unwavering support of friends and family always keeps you resilient.

Finally, **Secret Love** is an ode to unspoken affection for someone cherished deeply but never confessed. It tenderly captures hope that these emotions might one day find their voice.

So join us on this whimsical rollercoaster ride through memory lane. "**ALIVE**" isn't just a collection of poems; it's a time machine to rejuvenate your spirit and make you feel truly alive!

With all the giggles, tears, and endless gratitude.
Isha & Mahima

# Best Buddies

In the world of childhood with you and me
Tied in a friendship bond, forever to be.
Through games and giggles, we found our delight
Together with keeping our futures in sight.

Skinned knees and secrets we'd share
Amidst adventures wild, we did not care.
Growing up, life might change the trend
But you, my friend, are my childhood's best blend.



Isha

# Empty Hands

Made from embroidery floss
That half hitch knot
Enclosed on my wrist
Depicts that friendship exists

No monetary value
Yet cosmic glow
Promise of forever bond
Eternal you know

We grew up and met
On friendship day
Thought we were dumb
Celebrating this way

Those treasured moments
And friendship bands
Were not childish but exquisite
Says now my empty hands.



Mahima

# Reminiscence

In a home filled with joy,
A little girl's heart finds all to enjoy,
Creating memories with a family so dear
Full of dreams, laughters, and cheer.

Within those walls, a world did bloom,
With friends and dolls, a sacred room,
Their giggles echoed through the halls,
A bond that time could never disenthrall.

In the courtyard's warmth, they'd often play,
Indoor games and stories would fill the day,
With marble games and hide-and-seek,
In childhood's realm, they'd laugh and speak.

Amidst the aroma of spices that rise,
Her mother's love, a treasured prize,
In the kitchen's embrace, magic transpired,
A taste of heritage, her heart inspired.

Through sweltering summers, they'd find a way,
To splash in rivers and forget the day,
Mangoes sweet and ice cream delights,
A respite from the sun's relentless might.



Isha

In the quiet of night, as stars would gleam,
She'd whisper her dreams, like a secret stream,
With eyes closed tight, she'd reach for the skies,
Her aspirations soaring, as hope would rise.

From those cherished walls, she'd set her sight,
On dreams that danced in the moon's soft light,
A little girl, with wings unfurled,
Ready to paint the world, like an artist, pearled.

And as time drifts by, the girl has grown,
Yet, in that home, her heart finds its own,
For every memory woven within its core,
Forever a beacon to light her soul's encore.

So let the dreams of springhood whisper
What stays in the cold heart's crisper
The home where her love resides
A tapestry of memories that forever abides.



Isha

# Childhood Memories

In Jaipur, where the houses are pink,
My childhood home - a special link.
With friends, we'd play on the dusty streets
Marbles, kites, our laughter sweet.

Wonderful memories, a childhood home,
Sunsets painting domes, where memories roam.
Amidst the pink hues, laughter would ring,
In dusty streets, with friends, we'd swing.

Growing up in those narrow lanes,
Where memories of joy still remains.
Festivals and markets, full of cheer,
Our childhood stories started here.

Marbles clicked, kites soared high,
Amidst the warm winds, under the Rajasthan sky.
Growing up in corridors, secrets whispered loud,
A bond with friends, like a monsoon cloud.

Through festivals and markets, we'd explore,
The heartbeat of Jaipur, forevermore.
From those narrow lanes to futures unknown,
In the echoes of Jaipur, our stories have grown.



Isha

# Blossom of Youth

In adolescence's tender embrace we find
A girl on the cusp of change, her world unwinds.
Puberty's tempest and a sea of transformation,
Unfolding secrets of her body's creation.

Her reflection - a stranger in the mirror's gleam
As curves emerge and childhood is but a dream.
Her voice cracks; trembles in a newfound grace
As she steps forth to claim her rightful space.

Innocence wanes replaced by worldly cares
As her heart flutters, tangled in love's snares.
Emotions surge like waves upon the shore
A symphony of feelings she must explore.

With each new moon, a cycle blooms and starts
Nature's rhythm whispers in her beating heart.
Her body's wisdom - a mysterious guide
She learns to navigate the ebb and tide.

Amidst the changes, she seeks her own true voice
A journey inward, a personal choice.
With dreams as vast as the open sky,
She spreads her wings and learns to fly.



Isha

Yet, adolescence is a delicate terrain,
Where self-discovery can come with pain.
But from the struggles, strength begins to grow,
A woman blooms from the seeds she'll sow.

In the dance between girl and woman, she'll find,
A path to selfhood, both gentle and kind.
Puberty's tempest, a passage she'll brave,
Emerging stronger, with the power to save.

Through the labyrinth of adolescence, she'll
weave,
A tapestry of experiences, learning to believe.
In her heart's treasure chest, the key to her truth,
A girl's journey to womanhood, a courageous
sleuth.

# Growing Up

In the journey of growing up, something new
begins
A special time when a girl's adventure kicks in
It's called the first period - a natural part
A mix of feelings like a work of art.

Imagine a garden where flowers bloom
This is like a girl entering a special room
Her feelings are changing like day and night
A blend of emotions - a beautiful sight.

Just like a flower opens its petals wide
The first period brings feelings inside
It might be a bit confusing or strange
But it's a part of growing up, a natural change.



Isha

# Secret Love

Whisper of affections
I can never show
I will keep quiet
And you will never know.

Never meant to be tied
Were we in forever bond
It was not just love
But a way beyond.

Every word you uttered
Was deep and confident.
Falling in love
With your voice was evident.

Universe listened
To my plea; I agree
Our paths' crossing then
Was entirely Fate's decree.

The way you speak
The way you care
The way you listen
So sincere



Mahima

The way you understand
The way you explain
The purity in your eyes
Says you are a gentleman.

When I saw you
A story began to write
An unexpressed love
That I can't recite.

You belong to someone else
You can't be mine
This love is unattainable
My lips will confine.

You are a poem I penned down
But can never read aloud
An unspoken love
Profoundly endowed.

With time
Our journey fell apart
Your presence can never fade
From my heart.

I hope you remember me as I do
This secret love is pure and true.



Mahima

# We Found Love

That innocent smile
And ecstatic pure gaze
That mysterious eyes
Captured me in a maze.

Those enchanting talks
And unpretentious conventional ways
That filled my world
With radiant endless blaze.

That apology you asked
For a mistaken touch
I secretly smirk thought
You think too much.

That commitment and your presence
When I secretly sob
That gentle hug and those words
'I will be there whatever is the cause'.

Finally we entwined in the flawless sacred bond
We found love, not ordinary, but a way beyond.



Mahima

# A Fresh Dawn's Embrace

In the wreckage of a broken bond we stand,
Two souls once interlaced in love's embrace.
But now, we part, our separate ways unplanned,
To seek new beginnings in life's open space.

The weight of yesterday we cast aside,
A heavy burden now at last unbound.
In every tear that fell, a love denied
But hope and healing in each step we've found.

No longer bound by sorrow's heavy chains,
We rise, like phoenix from the ashes, free.
A vibrant world before us now remains,
A canvas painted with new destiny.

For in the darkest hour a truth is seen,
That in the breaking, new beginnings gleam.
The past dissolves like a memory's sweet sheen,
As life's rich mosaic, we dare to dream.

Let go, move forward in the dawn's warm glow,
Embrace the chance to heal, to bloom and to
grow.



Isha

# Life's Canvas

Life is like a painting we create,
Colors of joy challenges we face.
Sunsets and sunrises, highs and lows,
We keep going; our story unfolds.

Storms may come, clouds may go
But inside, a strong heart does grow.
In this short time, joy and strife,
We paint our existence - the masterpiece of life.



Isha

# Big Fat Wedding

Lavish green garden
And plates full of waste
Two birds were brought
Into the nest

While they made their way
Towards the crowd
All eyes turned to them
The cheering noise was loud

With all the add ons
And artificial glow
It was not a knot
Not less than a show

With all the show off
The hosts got applause
Deep inside they knew
It was a perpetual loss

Day passed by
And lights faded away
Love struggled all along
To find its own way



Mahima

# Bridging Worlds

In a land of frost, she stood alone
Her heart is a tapestry of hues unknown.
From Ganges' banks to the Northern lights,
She ventured brave forth on new flights.

Her footsteps whispered tales untold
Of spices, saris, and marigold.
Yet, in this place of snow and pine,
A new beginning she'd define.

She longed for songs from childhood days
For fragrant air, and vibrant plays.
Her parents' voices- soft and kind,
Echoed in the depths of her mind.

Friends left behind like distant stars,
She yearned for laughter and familiar bars.
Through letters penned and phone calls made,
Their love, a lifeline, would never fade.

She'd close her eyes and they'd appear,
In dreams that brought them ever closer.
Yet, as the seasons turned and changed,
A transformation arrived - deep and strange.



Isha

Through maple leaves and prairie winds,
A fusion of worlds, a journey begins.
She learned to dance on frozen ground,
To let her heart in both worlds be found.

With every step, a bridge she'd build,
Her past and present are gently skilled.
In the land of snow and maple trees,
She found a home, she found her ease.

Through shared cuisines and stories spun,
A new family formed, a new life began.
Canada's embrace, so wide and warm,
Wrapped around her like a comforting arm.

Her roots took hold, both deep and high,
Beneath the northern sky's vast sigh.
Every snowflake reflects a glimpse of her story,
A tale of courage, strength, and glory.

So, let this tale forever stand,
Of a woman bold who dared to land
In a foreign world, she made her stand,
Bridging worlds, heart in hand.



Isha

# Echoes of Home:
# A Song of Longing

In the depths of my soul,
A longing does reside
For a place I once called home,
Where my heart does confide.

But now it's a distant memory,
A dream I can't reclaim
A whisper in the night
A distant and haunting name.

The scent of my mother's kitchen
The warmth of her embrace,
The laughter of my cousins
Each with smiles on their face.

These memories of home
They cling to me like dust
In the corners of my mind,
In the people I still trust.

Oh, how the heart does ache
Like a song without an end,
For the place I can't return to
My home, my dearest friend.



Isha

The streets I used to wander
The trees I used to climb,
Now they exist in reverie
Frozen in the sands of time.

There was old mango tree in the backyard
With branches reaching high,
Where I'd sit and ponder life
Beneath the endless blue sky.

Its leaves whispered secrets
And its roots ran deep and strong,
But now it's just a memory,
Where I no longer belong.

The streets are not the same
They've lost their youthful sheen,
The houses stand as sentinels
Guarding what has been.

The people I once knew
They've scattered far and wide,
The friends I left behind
Have all moved with the tide.



Isha

Each night when I close my eyes
I'm transported back,
To the place that lives within me
And the memories I unpack.

I hear the distant laughter
Echoing down the hall,
I can see my father's smile,
The bravest of all.

The taste of homemade pudding
The scent of freshly-cut grass,
These are the things that in my heart
That shall forever amass.

For though I cannot return
To the realm where I was born,
These memories are my compass
On life's windy, recurring morn.

This longing grips me like a vice,
It squeezes and it pains,
For the home that's far away
Forever in my heart remains.



Isha

The years may come and go
Like a river's ceaseless flow,
But the love for my dear home
Shall eternally continue to glow.

Nostalgia paints the walls
Of the canvas of my mind,
A masterpiece of love and loss
Coated with the laughter of a child.

I yearn to turn the clock
And find my way back there
To breathe the air of yesteryears,
To feel that tender care.

But time is like a river
Forever onward bound,
My home's now in a distant island
Where I can't be found.

So I'll carry it within me
Like a torch against the dark,
A guiding light to lead me home
With a never-fading spark.



Isha

In the stillness of the night
In the silence of my soul,
I'll cherish those dear memories,
Where my heart found its goal.

For home is not a place
But a feeling deep and true,
A love that lives forever
In the depths of me and you.

And though I cannot return
To the home I hold so dear,
I'll carry it within me
Through every smile and tear.

For in the tapestry of life
Wherever I may roam,
I'll find my way back home
In the echoes of this poem.



Isha

# A Daughter's Love Across the Seas

In the hushed corners of my heart's cavern,
A flickering flame of nostalgia burns
For the bond we shared, so rare and so divine,
A father's love, a daughter's lifeline.

But now, across the oceans wide
I stand alone feeling the ache inside,
For you, dear father, are far away,
In a distant land, where you must stay.

The memories we made etched in my mind,
Of laughter and tears, of stories intertwined,
Your guiding hand that led me through,
Every storm and challenge that I knew.

Oh! How I miss your warm embrace,
The strength you gave me; it can't be replaced,
Your words of wisdom echo in my ears,
Whispering solace amidst my fears.

The scent of your cologne still lingers near
Transporting me back to a time so dear,
Where your presence filled every room
Radiating love, dispelling gloom.



Isha

Though distance separates our souls
The love we share forever holds
A bond unbreakable, forged in time,
A daughter's love for her father, sublime.

So, father dear, from afar I send
My love, my prayers, my every trend.
May the stars guide you and keep you safe
As I navigate this foreign space.

For in my heart, you'll always be
The strength I lean on eternally
And as I count the days until we meet,
I'll cherish the memories; bittersweet.



Isha

# Mothers and Daughters

In a world full of love and care,
There is a bond so strong, beyond compare.
A connection that time won't sever -
The joy of a mother and daughter forever.

From the very first day, a love so pure
A precious bond that time will endure.
Through laughter, tears, and everything,
A mother's love is an eternal spring.

From morning talks to late-night chats,
Secret whispers and gentle pats
The wisdom shared, the lessons taught:
A mother's love is a treasure sought.

Through childhood days and teenage years,
Navigating life's joys and fears.
A guiding hand, a listening ear:
A mother's love is always near.

Through ups and downs, thick and thin,
A mother's love is a constant within.
In every milestone, big or small,
A mother's love is the greatest of all.



Isha

The laughter shared, the memories made,
A mother's love is an everlasting braid.
In reminiscing moments, we find delight:
A mother's love is shining so bright.

For even as time moves along,
The bond we share grows ever strong.
A timeless connection, filled with grace:
A mother's love is a cherished embrace.

So let us celebrate this love so grand,
A mother and daughter, hand in hand.
In cheerful nostalgia, we shall sing,
Of a bond unbreakable, that forever brings.



Isha

# Grandparents

I am looking at your picture
A white garland it wears

Every frame depicts the wisdom
Gained through the years

Time has turned your hairs gray
Eyes still hold memories of each day

A path is mapped with every wrinkle
There is a story behind every crinkle

Your unconditional love
That you never expressed

When you were there -
I was truly blessed.

How could I accept
That we will never meet?

The day you were gone
I couldn't sleep.

Tears in my eyes
And shivering with fear.



Mahima

Will I be able to see you again?
That abruptly you did disappear.

I felt you sitting near me
I asked why
How could you just leave
Without a goodbye?

The journey is long
Without you I can't survive
I cried my heart out
I don't want to be alive

You said,
"This unpredictable life
Can not be planned
Always pray for happiness
Lend helping hand
Be honest, speak truth
Walk the right lane
Keep your values high
You will win the game

From this mortal body
My soul will release
You have my blessing
Let me rest in peace"



Mahima

Now,
Nobody waits for the dawn of my day
Nobody understands silence and hear what I say
Nobody consoles my heart that quietly weeps
Nobody recites stories, so that I can sleep
Nobody answers the insane questions I ask
Nobody I can trust, everyone wears a mask
Nobody knows the battle I fought
See, I have become what you always taught

Trying to forge my way as life is crucible
Tired of fighting alone, RIP I say:
Return If Possible.



Mahima

# Celebration of Womanhood

In the embrace of womanhood we stand
A sisterhood of strength hand in hand.
Cherishing the essence that makes us unique
A force of nature - powerful and mystique.

Embrace your curves, your flaws, your grace,
For in your reflection, it shows a beautiful face.
A heart that beats with courage and might
A spirit that soars while taking flight.

Love being a woman with all that you are
In your journey, you'll surely go a lot far.
Celebrate your wisdom, your dreams, your voice,
For within you lies the power of choice.

Lift your fellow women, their battles, their
dreams,
In unity, we're stronger, or so it seems.
Support their endeavors, their hopes, their strife,
For together, we create a vibrant life.

No competition, no envy, no disdain,
In our hearts, let empathy reign.
Embrace diversity, and let kindness grow,
In this sisterhood, we all can glow.



Isha

In nurturing others, we nurture ourselves
A bond of love like a treasure on our shelves.
Let the world witness our unity's grace,
A community of women in every place.

So, love being a woman, strong and free
In unity, we shape our destiny.
Support your sisters on this earthly ride
In womanhood's embrace, we stand side by side.



Isha

# From Bump to Toddler Steps: A Mother's Journey

In the quiet of the night, I felt a flutter
A secret bond; a love so pure, I couldn't utter.
A tiny miracle in a life about to start
As you grew within me and my beating heart.

Through the months you kicked with glee,
I cherished each moment between you and me.
My body transformed, my heart filled with grace
As I eagerly awaited to look at your tiny face.

Then came the day when you arrived with a cry
Tears of joy welled up as I held you high.
A newborn's scent, a soft and tender sigh
Leaving you incapacitated I'd never say goodbye.

Your fingers so delicate, your eyes so bright
I watched you grow all day and night.
From the first smile to those foremost steps,
My heart swelled with love in every depth.

But time...it flew faster than a breeze
As you moved from a baby to a toddler with ease.
I miss those sleepless nights and cuddles so warm
Yet I'm grateful for every phase, every storm.



Isha

From those first words to your curious mind
To the endless laughter your spirit intertwined.
The journey of motherhood - a bittersweet ride,
I cherish it all with you by my side.

Now you're a toddler exploring the world anew,
And though I miss those baby days, it's true,
I look forward to every milestone yet to come
With you, my darling, my precious one.

So, as I reminisce, I hold you near
Whispering tales of your journey, my dear.
From pregnancy's glow to toddlerhood's embrace
Forever in my heart, you'll have your special place.



Isha

# Sometimes

Sometimes..
Hope is suppressed
Dreams seem unrealistic
Belief is backpaddled
Plans take a wrong turn
Tears are not the happy ones

Sometimes...
Doubt clutches
Trust shatters
Patience saturates
Blessings struggle
And reality is unacceptable

Sometimes..
Chaos is within
Battles are surrendered
Truth is confined
Silence makes noise
Ethics loose voice

Sometimes...
Principles seem bookish
Integrity is interrogated
Authenticity stifled
Prayers are unheard
Questions are unanswered



Mahima

Sometimes..
There are times when life is a complete mess
With phases lived but inexpressible by nature
Also moments we miss when memories rupture
Remember all times will be 'some time'  in future.



Mahima

# Silence

Shadows of silence and emotions untold
Torrent of pain that time cannot hold

Silent house, silent people, in motives to maneu-
ver
That haunting silence even now does devour

Anxiety grip, relentless agony, I find despair
Darkness bring tear of Anguish with nightmare

Everyday I wear a firm disguise
An innocent smile on my face used to suffice

Invisible battle I was fighting alone
I tried but they pretended to be unknown

The truth was buried and voice suppressed
Hope stifled and soul oppressed

Silence then became my shield
I kept quiet and lies concealed

I put my pride aside, feelings did subside
Silence is a venom when no one is beside



Mahima

Insomnia had kept me awake
My pillow knows the tear I shed
Every night I confronted
The empty side of my bed.

I was a bird with a broken wing
Shattered by what I have seen

Within the wall of deception, I was confined
In invisible shackles were spirit, heart and mind

Tired of fake smile, silence and lie
I gave up and it's time to say goodbye

I prayed, Lord, please free my spirit
Screaming to the sky, I said, 'I quit'

Was it an oracle or my inner voice
Told me your life is always your choice

Life gives you emotional bashes
Be pheonix that rise from ashes

Fear decline, silence break
Wiped my tear, warrior awake

It was a time to find my soul
Find missing me and take a step towards my goal.

 Mahima

Happiness and Hope inextricably intertwined my heart
I was ready for a new beginning chance to restart

I was embracing the
sunrise, life and fate
Reincarnated in the same birth
I will win, I anticipate

I was healing finding peace
And i was free
I loved myself as
I was not cheating on me

I don't live in past
Fussing about wrong
I forgive myself for
Not being strong
Word of gratitude for those
Who accepted me the way I am
Thank you for trusting me and
Telling me I will and I cam
There is not arrogance, ego
Or any race
Nevertheless, self respect is a humble grace

Emotional storm takes time to settle
I proudly carry the scar of battle.

                    Mahima

# Karma and Forgiveness

When I walk through the memory lane
Cicatrix of wretchedness still remain

The person in the mirror I daily meet
I never did lie and never cheat

Honesty was an expensive gift I offered
Loyalty betrayed, In silence I suffered

I was torn deep within
Fighting against my own kin

Who am I, where do I belong
Why only me and what went wrong

Lots of questions for which answers I seek
In history's rhyme, I found a guidance deep

The wheel of time never forbidden
In Karma's ledger deeds are written

For every intend consequences are due
Universe listens and echoes what you do



Mahima

In the realm of Karma, intentions hold
Justice is done and truth is unfold

Embracing the truth, I shall stride
No fear of judgment, and emotions I won't hide

I am not a pawn, I am ready to speak
Remember, what you sow, so shall you reap

In the end the visor will fade
Revealing the truth of masquerade

A liar's prestige build on fragile ground
Web of deceit spun will eventually be found

The mental trauma and pain prolonged-
What doesn't kills you makes you strong

Annals of time gave me a mentor profound
Who said perform your duty and be role bound

He endowed me a life's insight
I forgive, but if needed I am ready to fight

Seek no fruit of action, he did declare
The tales of Karma are inked with care



Mahima

Staying detached from the result makes you
whole
The truth is wrapped with your immortal soul

With the grace of forgiveness, I shall heal
I will live in peace and let Karma deal.



Mahima

# Hope

I am still questioned my every move
How many times do I need to prove?

Those nights were suffocating
And days went silent
Each minute heavier than before
On lonely paths where hope was no more

I ask them who still doubt and accuse
How many miles have you walked in my shoes?

Heart that bruised by wounds of words
Somber note of a trapped bird
Every line I wrote in the diary
Soliloquy of pain, expressed silently

I gathered the shards of my own shattered soul
How many times did you support?

There was a girl who smiled all the time
To show the world that she is fine
So called sacred bond was torn apart
One by one everyone depart

Now your voice muffled and your heart melts
Where were you when I asked for help



Mahima

Now open your ears and listen quietly

Problems never made me strong
I dragged myself out of the place where I never
belong
I am not sorry and I have no regrets
It was not my fault and I was never wrong

I was hurt and I was broken
I can not fly and might not run
Friends supported and Family became ladder
I still have hope and miles to toddle
I still have hope and miles to toddle...

                                    Mahima

# I Found Happiness

With the silhouette buildings and blue sky
With quiet dawn and luminous sunrise
With fresh air and singing of birds
With rustling leaves and nature's surprise
I found happiness.

With a cup of coffee and turning pages
In the quiet of library and captivating ways
With imaginary characters or knowledgeable
roots
In the bibliosmia of new books
I found happiness.

When elders bless and strangers smile
When tears of joy and laughters on faces compile
Neither in grand venture nor in chaotic inclusion
In solace of sacred places and in divine seclusion
I found happiness.

With blooming flowers and whispering trees
With the vast ocean and tranquil beach
In the dense forest and gentle river
With twinkling star as cosmos uncover
I found happiness.

 Mahima

In budget travels or with luxurious touch
In backpacking trips or religious clutch
In solo adventures or weekend getaways
In domestic destination or international ways
I found happiness.

I found happiness everywhere
In stories I lived and scar I wear
I found my voice, my faith, my flame
In the journey called life, I am my name.



Mahima

# Moments to Relish: Me Time

In the busy swirl of life, we often forget
The need to pause, to take a quiet breath.
Amid the daily grind in a moment's grace
To find our center in life's hectic race.

For in those moments, we find our own
A chance to breathe and to be alone.
To recharge, to simply just be
In the daily hustle, we find 'me.'

The world can wait, the rush can slow,
In 'me time,' our inner selves can grow.
A pause to reflect, to find our way,
In the chaos of life awaits a brighter day.

So don't forget in your daily routine
To take a pause in life's busy scene.
In 'me time,' you'll discover, you'll find
The quiet moments and a peace of mind.



Isha

# Day with Nature

The birds were chirping in their nest
I woke up with a smile as the air caressed

A gentle breeze blew making the trees dance
On the calm sea, a blue reflection does glance

There were birds flying way too high
Testifying the limit as the soaring sky

Waves continually hitting the rock
Taught me not to give up and never stop

See the sun hides behind the cloud
The orange glow make me vowed

Then the nature displayed a different show
Asking me to keep pace, don't go slow

Finding myself drenched in the rain
Serenity I felt, free from all inner pain

Smelling fresh dewy petrichor on the land
I never wanted the day to end



Mahima

It is true, everything that comes has to leave
But right now I want the time to freeze

The day with nature calmed down my soul
Motivating me towards my life's goal.



Mahima

# Being You

I am a fearless kid
Driving through the skid
I laugh, behave insane
And I crack jokes that are lame
Break me with your bitter lie
I am a bird, I am born to fly.

I will wake up, dress up
Fall and again try
I will be silent or loud
Keep quiet or shout
Shoot me with your words
But you can't ignore
I am a lioness, I am born to roar.

I will dance in rain
Laugh in pain
Call me crazy, my feelings absurd
Label me by any name bewildered
Knock me down
With all the hate, but it's my time
I am a star, I am born to shine.

 Mahima

Let them judge,
I know how my story will manifest
Life gives you pain
But it leads to a new life's quest.

I just want to say...

It is not how you high you shine
It is not about whether you fly
It's not about the name
Neither about the fame
It's not about the desire
Nor the feats you aspire
It's not about how much you earn
It's not about learnings you yearn
It's not about the sufferings true
Not either about the beauty you view
It's not about the brain
Not anyone of the gain.

You are divine and pure
Flawless, epitome of love.
You are perfect, smart, and
Immaculate creation of God.



Mahima

You are invincible, confident,
Powerful and strong
You are undefeated, unbeaten
Yet unpretentious
Making you winner by default.

Remember you are blessed!
You may be in the queue
It's all about that smile
And you just being you.



Mahima

# Wandering Girl

With every travel, a tale unfolds
A passport stamped with stories told.

With friends, family or strangers, moments we
cheer
Every picture has a secret anecdote to share.

New places, cultures and traditions so rich
Every new face has its own story to pitch.

Sunrise on beaches and sunset on plain
A fresh petrichor from the pattern of rain.

Mountains stands tall, and majestic, and might
Peaks touching the sky, and eye catching its sight.

Vast oceans they are, limitlessly deep
Beautiful undiscovered world, secrets it keep.

The quant cafe and bustling of street
The aroma of coffee and new world we meet.

In the depth of silence, tranquility I embrace
I get whispering answers miles far from my place.

 Mahima

I earn lifetime memories
The moments that I always cheer
With joy, laugh, cry and all emotions
The story will echo for years.

I keep traveling exploring the world
I wish journey continue to unfurl
I hope more unknown destinations reveal
I love to be called a wandering girl.



Mahima

# About the Authors

Mahima Gupta, a native of the vibrant city of Jaipur, embarked on her poetic journey early in life, with her first poem published in a Hindi newspaper while she was in the 6th grade.

She holds an M.Tech degree and currently works for a multinational company in Bangalore. An accomplished athlete, she has been selected for Basketball Nationals and has competed at the district level in swimming.

Mahima is a firm believer in the power of continuous learning and growth. Nature provides her with profound healing, and her writing is deeply inspired by her personal experiences and the lessons they have taught her. Her debut poetry collection, "Alive," offers readers a unique blend of personal insights and solace. Through her poems, she shares her journey of trials and triumphs.

Looking to the future, Mahima intends to delve deeper into the lessons from her experiences and the magical blessings and profound influence of the Almighty.

# About the Authors

Isha Shingari, born and raised in the culturaly rich city of Jaipur, holds a doctorate in Computer Science. An esteemed professor, she imparts her knowledge with passion and dedication. Beyond the realm of academia, Dr. Isha finds solace in the rhythmic world of poetry, where she explores the depths of human emotion and experience.

Her poetry collection reflects her life's journey, capturing the essence of childhood memories, the unbreakable bond between mothers and daughters, and the myriad facets of womanhood. Through her verses, Dr. Shingari weaves a tapestry of nostalgia, family, life, victory and hope, inviting readers to reflect on their own lives and find beauty in the everyday moments being more ALIVE!

In her spare time, Dr. Shingari enjoys immersing herself in nature, cherishing quiet moments of self-reflection, and drawing inspiration from the world around her. Her work is a testament to the power of words and the enduring strength of the human spirit.

# ALIVE

A journey through verses

MAHIMA GUPTA
ISHA SHINGARI